Haunts of the Halifax Slasher

A walk through hysteria and violence
in a Pennine milltown

Tim Chapman

Haunts of the Halifax Slasher
by Tim Chapman

Parts of this book were first published by Strange Attractor Press, 2005. This edition published in 2020.

Copyright © 2005, 2020 Tim Chapman

All rights reserved.

ISBN: 9798619293555

No part of this book may be reproduced in any form or by any electronic or mechanical means including information storage and retrieval systems, without the express written permission of the publisher. The only exception is by a reviewer, who may quote short excerpts in a review.

CONTENTS

Haunts of the Halifax Slasher (2005)   7

Old haunts revisited (2019)   47

Ballad of the Halifax Slasher   58

All Halifax history depends on Halifax geography.

> Phyllis Bentley

Black Halifax boiled in phosphorus.

> Ted Hughes

For a journey through hysteria, mob violence, murder and fascism, it's as well to start from a place of calm.

Savile Park, the green heart of polite life to the south of the town centre, a tamed moorland for sport and strolls. The land, then known as Skircoat Moor, was gifted to the Halifax Corporation in 1866 by the Savile family, lords of the manor since the 14th century, with the proviso it remained unenclosed for the benefit of the public, forever.

At the top, the northern renaissance solidity of the Crossley and Porter Orphanage now provides education to the town's brightest children: in season, the park is planted with football and rugby posts. Beyond that, the gothic rocket of the Wainhouse Tower stretches to its rococo crown, an eccentric sentry keeping watch over the town and giving the architectural finger to any approaching traveller. Even from the grass of the park, you can look over the steep encircling valleys to other hills beyond. Some bright days, it can feel like the top of the world.

Unless you know, it doesn't feel like a place of murder. On 4 April 1979, Josephine Anne Whitaker was walking home from her grandparents, across the park at midnight. She was 19, working at the town's eponymous building society, living with her mum and step-dad. She was found dead the next morning, head smashed with a hammer and stabbed 25 times, left lying by the wall around the school. She was the eleventh known victim of the Yorkshire Ripper, Peter Sutcliffe.

Assistant Chief Constable George Oldfield sounded the warning the next day, as police began interviewing some 5,000 townsfolk: "Anyone could be the next victim. This was a savage attack on an innocent young woman. Clearly we have a homicidal maniac at large – a man obviously mentally ill."

It wasn't the first time that Halifax lived in fear of such a maniac. In November 1938, the town was plunged into panic by the attacks of an unseen assailant known only as the Halifax Slasher. Women were cut with razors; right-thinking men patrolled the streets; bystanders who looked a bit odd were beaten up; it was two weeks of terror of a kind said to have been unseen since the days of Jack the Ripper. The difference was that in 1979, as in 1888, it was real – all too bloody real. In 1938, the verdict was mass hysteria. The Halifax Slasher simply never existed.

In 1938, Savile Park looked different. Britain knew it was on the brink of war, and volunteers had already dug trenches on the park for air raid shelters. The government line was still appeasement of Nazi Germany – a policy hatched between Hitler and Chamberlain's foreign secretary, Lord Halifax, at a meeting over 17–21 November 1937, exactly one year before the beginning of the Slasher panic.

On 30 September 1938, Chamberlain returned from Munich and delivered his lines: "I believe it is peace for our time. Go home and get a nice quiet sleep." By November, local novelist Phyllis Bentley was writing to the *Yorkshire Post* to denounce this appeasement – afterwards, she later recalled, "some Halifax shopkeepers... murmured in my ear their thanks."

And on the nights of the ninth and tenth in Germany, the November Pogrom – Kristallnacht. Broken glass, mobs on the street, beating up the alien.

Many of the key locations in the short reign of the Halifax Slasher can be visited on a short walk through west Halifax. Begin by heading up the park, past the school, under the shadow of the Wainhouse Tower.

This dark stone folly, rising some 75 metres above an overgrown cemetery, was erected by John Edward Wainhouse in the 1870s. It was meant to serve as a chimney for the dyeworks he'd inherited on Washer Lane, some 100 metres further down the valley slope. The dyeworks were sold off before construction was complete, and Wainhouse had the octagonal structure topped by an ornate observatory, reached by 369 steps winding around the chimney flue. Some reckon this was his intention all along – to build himself a platform where he could overlook the estate of a local rival. Some versions of the story say Wainhouse wanted to spy on his rival's wife. Some give his monument the name of the Tower of Spite.

From the top of the park, the ground drops down past the brick windows of the squat methodist church to the King Cross junction, where half a dozen roads spider across a vertiginous topography. On his travels for *An English Journey* in 1933, JB Priestley – born in Bradford, almost a local boy – declared the town's terrain the hilliest of any town of its size in England: "factories and rows of houses seem to be sticking up and out at all mad angles... a grim, craggy place."

The first road to the left drops down to Sowerby Bridge, then out along the Ryburn valley to Ripponden. It was there, some six miles away from the dense terraces of Halifax, that the Slasher terror had its prologue.

In the early evening of 16 November 1938, Gertie Watts and Mary Gledhill, both 21-year-old mill workers, were walking down Old Bank Lane from their Barkisland home to an evening class in Ripponden below. Halfway down the long, unlit path, they heard some slight noise behind them and were immediately hit by something like a mallet or hatchet. The girls struggled with their unseen assailant before escaping back up the hill, blood streaming from wounds to their heads. They reached a cottage owned by Mr and Mrs Harold Helliwell and lapsed into shock. Mr Helliwell briefly searched for their attacker but failed to locate him. The girls remembered that they had seen a man of around 30–40 years of age when leaving Barkisland, dressed in a soft overcoat, cap pulled down low over his forehead; and again by the Fleece Inn. They reckoned he was the attacker.

Reports of the attack on the Barkisland girls, coupled with the murder of eight-year-old Phyllis Hirst in Bradford a few weeks earlier, meant that fears ran high. *The Halifax Daily Courier and Guardian*: "Until the culprit is found and effectively dealt with, there is not likely to be much peace of mind, not only at Barkisland

and Ripponden, but further afield. In the local district, at any rate, the affair has created a tremendous sensation, and it has thoroughly upset the people." The seeds had been planted for the Slasher panic that began just five days later.

Cross over the junction to King Cross Road, and along past the disembodied spire of St Paul's Church. Now, as in the 1930s, you move from the bourgeois homes round Savile Park into the lower class area around Queens Road. This is the spine of west Halifax, a community of mills and terraces. The Wainhouse Tower watches over the road's long stretch, though its view in 1938 would have been obscured by choking smog.

The factories were busy then and unemployment was low thanks largely to the local machine tool trade, booming with rearmament orders. The red brick factory inscribed "Mackintosh's Chocolate Works 1898" marks another native industry, created by John Mackintosh, the toffee king. His son Harold Vincent, later Viscount Mackintosh, was a director of the Halifax Building Society and brought traditional Yorkshire penny consciousness to the War effort as chairman of the National Savings Committee.

The chocolate works now houses the Pennywise Enterprise Discount Centre, selling to the new Queens Road locals. In the 1950s, Mirpuri migrant workers from the Kashmir were shipped into Halifax to work the night shifts at the mills, and the community rooted itself here.

Now, the few open shops sell saris and spices. The cars parked along the street carry "Come on England" world cup stickers next to dangling Islamic symbols, but the fact that "the Pakis" dare to remain now the mill jobs have gone seems to be an affront to some in the town. During the Slasher panic, this was a close-knit community with deep suspicions of strangers. It still can be.

Other outsiders also made their home here. The Holy Protection Ukrainian Catholic Church looms over the street, a former Methodist chapel now garnished with black marble plaques marking the millennium of Prince Volodymyr the Great and the 1933 genocide. Other buildings are inscribed with a more respectably Victorian past – the Constitutional Club, the Kingston Liberal Club 1894 and the Halifax Joint Stock Banking Co Ltd, now warehouses for discount furniture, carpets and wallpaper.

Opposite the Joint Stock Banking Co on the corner of Gibbet Street is the former School of Art, now Queens Road Neighbourhood Centre. Jasper Street, on the far side of this, was the scene of the attack that gave the Halifax Slasher his name.

On the evening of 24 November 1938, Clayton Aspinall stood in a doorway facing the School of Art across Jasper Street. Aspinall was the caretaker of St Andrew's Methodist Sunday School and was looking out for latecomers to the evening meetings. As he waited, a youngish man ran down from his right, from Arundel Street. Aspinall: "Naturally I had no reason to suspect that anything was unusual. The man came towards me on the footpath and as he reached me I stood back a little to let him pass, but in passing he struck out. I put up my right arm to guard against the blow. My spectacles were disturbed, and in bothering to catch them, I just missed seeing the immediate movement of the man. But he ran through the School of Art side gateway, went around the back of the school, and out of sight."

The police soon arrived on the scene, but could find no trace of the attacker, whom Aspinall described as 5'9", aged around 30, in a fawn overcoat with a slight stoop and "well-brushed hair inclined to ginger". He seemed to be local, noted the *Courier*: "No stranger could thread his way in semi-darkness around the rear of the School of Art or the maze of semi-private streets all around. Police vigilance has not been relaxed."

The main concern was for the female students of the School of Art – lessons were held behind locked doors, and the students left in groups or under escort. Tensions were already high, and two girls were found to be carrying a police whistle and a pepperpot to defend themselves against attack. The next day's banner headline in the *Courier* gave a name to the menace, a name that gave it some new reality: "£10 Police Reward for Arrest of Halifax 'Slasher'".

Another story in the same day's paper is suggestive. Under the headline "Why we gossip":

"The tattler generally suffers from an itch to attract attention and to see people interestedly hanging on her words. She – it is generally a 'she' – feels a sense of importance when all ears are strained to catch whatever it is she has to say. The temptation to tell as thrilling a tale as possible becomes irresistible."

Tensions were high before the attack on Aspinall because of an assault just a few streets away a few days earlier.

Turn down Gibbet Street, named for the town's infamous engine of execution, to Francis Street, a residential lane overshadowed by the dark hulk of the Park United Reformed Church and the golden spire of the Park Congregational Church. This latter church has a murder of its own – in September 1953, the battered body of six-year-old Mary Hackett was found buried in the foundations, six weeks after she went missing from her home in Cemetery Lodge. The caretaker of the church, Albert George Hall, was hanged for her murder, protesting his innocence to the last.

Fifteen years earlier on 21 November, Mary Sutcliffe, a 21-year-old worker at Mackintosh's Queens Road factory, was returning home from the late shift along Francis Street.

As she was about to cross Lister Lane, an unfamiliar man stepped out from under a street light with his arm raised. Sutcliffe instinctively threw up her hand and ran to her home on Allerton Street, now vanished under industrial units. There she found her wrist was bleeding from a deep, clean cut like that inflicted by a razor. The cut required four stitches.

Sutcliffe described her attacker as aged 25–35, 5'11", with a battered, double-breasted military raincoat over a dark grey suit, and soft trilby. His eyes seemed somewhat more prominent than usual.

Eight evenings later, Sutcliffe was attacked again on the doorstep of her home. This time, she was just leaving for the night shift – her mother had barely seen Mary out the door when she heard a thud and a scream. Mary lay in the yard, with a cut through her clothing and across her chest.

Back on Gibbet Street, the history of violence continues as you descend into town, past the overgrown General Cemetery and the newer Madni Mosque next door, where Mohammed Haji Sultan, general secretary of the mosque, was attacked in May 1999 by six men wearing balaclavas and carrying iron bars. The shop on the corner of Back Rhodes Street was the scene of an unsolved murder in 1957. On 8 June, Whitsuntide Saturday, the body of 80-year-old shopkeeper Emily Pye was found by her niece, battered to death with a fireside companion set. Detectives from Scotland Yard were called in and 9,500 local men quizzed, with no arrests.

Still further down, on the corner of Bedford Street North, sits the fulcrum of bloody Halifax. The gibbet itself, one corner of the fearsome triangle of the Beggar's Litany: "From Hell, Hull and Halifax, Good Lord deliver us." The phrase is usually attributed to John Taylor's seventeenth century doggerel, *A very merrie wherrie*, but this only preserves an older prayer for protection from harsh justice. The Halifax Gibbet dates back to at least 1286, when John of Dalton became the first victim of the Earl of Warren's royalty to execute thieves.

Occasional vandalism permitting, a modern replica of the gibbet now stands on the reconstructed platform. An outline phallus in rough wood, it is a rude prototype of the engine popularised by Doctor Joseph-Ignace Guillotin (born, by some small pattern of date, in 1738). Rather than the angled blade of the French device, a surprisingly small curved axe held in a lead-weighted slab of wood did the business here.

The Halifax Gibbet Law set out the simple rule: "That if a Felon be taken within their Liberty, with Goods stoln out or within the Liberty or Precincts of the said Forest [of Hardwick], either Hand-habend, Backberand or Confessand, Cloth or any other commodity of the value of Thirteen Pence half-penny, that they shall after three Markets or Meeting Days, within the Town of Hallifax, next after such his Apprehension, and being condemned, he shall be taken to the Gibbet and there shall have his Head cut off from his Body."

Beheadings took place at the main Saturday markets, ensuring a good turn out; the condemned was daily placed in stocks in the meanwhile. Audience participation was encouraged. According to Raphael Holinshead's *Chronicle* of 1587, the axe was set in motion by the removal of a pin, to which a long rope was attached:

"Every man there present doth take hold of the rope or putteth forth his arm so near to the same as he can get in token that he is willing to see justice executed, and pulling out the pin in this manner the head-block wherein the axe is fashioned doth fall down with such violence that if the neck of the transgressor were as big as a bull it should be cut in sunder and roll from the body by an huge distance.

"If it be so that the offender be apprehended for an ox, sheep or kine, or any such cattle, the self beast, or other of its kind shall have the end of the rope tied into them so that they being driven to draw out the pin whereby the offender is executed."

There are no records for much of the gibbet's reign, with the first recorded execution after John of Dalton being one Charles Haworth on 15 January 1539. Despite the draconian reputation, the official record claims only 63 executions until the end of the gibbet's use in 1650. The register of victims is a roll call of local surnames: Crabtree, Appleyard, Fairbank, Illingworth, Clegg; and no fewer than three Sutcliffes, in 1591, 1623 and 1629. And on the first of January 1542: "Unidentified stranger".

Halifax's association with beheadings is even older. By local legend, the town's very name is derived from such a capital crime. *Brewer's Dictionary of Phrase and Fable* says of Halifax:

"That is, halig fax or holy hair. Its previous name was Horton. The story is that a certain clerk of Horton, being jilted, murdered his quondam sweetheart by cutting off her head, which he hung in a yew-tree. The head was looked on with reverence, and came to be regarded as a holy relic. In time it rotted away, leaving little filaments or veins spreading out between the bark and body of the tree like fine threads. These filaments were regarded as the fax or hair of the murdered maiden."

Another version puts a different spin on the relationship. Aelred, the hermit-like priest of the chapel of St John the Baptist, became father confessor to a young girl from a nearby convent, and performed due flagellations for his thoughts of her and her golden hair. One day, the girl confessed that she had met a godly man for whom her passions raged. "Satan, I know thee, and I defy thee!" Aelred rather presumptuously cried, and swiftly removed the temptress' head from her body.

Another legend derives the name from "Holy face" and claims some portion of the physiognomy of John the Baptist, after its removal by the whim of the jilted Salome, was buried beneath the Parish Church. The saint's head does appear on Halifax's coat of arms, along with a paschal lamb, but the town's name more likely comes from the Old English *Halh Gefeaxe* – a hollow of coarse grass.

The gibbet may also have inspired a more recent death, one mentioned in WG Sebald's novel of memory and Nazi-era tragedy, *Austerlitz*. On 13 October 1999, a local handyman named Colin Vincent beheaded himself with what the newspapers called a home-made guillotine. Vincent had constructed the device in the stairwell of his outside cellar door at Cheltenham Place, to the south-east of the town centre, following the death of his wife from cancer. Police found a spirit level near the body, presumably to check the engine was true before it was set in action; and, in Vincent's hand, the pliers he'd used to cut a restraining wire to drop the blade.

It seems inevitable that the Slasher should strike in the shadow of the gibbet, although in 1938 the base stood bare. On the evening of 27 November, Beatrice Sorrell, a 19-year-old warehouse hand, parted with her older lover, Michael Alphonsius Higgins and walked down Bedford Street North, past a dark yard. As she told it: "I suddenly saw an arm come out. The arm was mackintoshed, and the hand seemed to be covered with a white handkerchief. I felt a sharp dig, and I said 'Oh, oh.' I was too terrified to scream properly. I saw no person properly, and running under a lamp found my arm was bleeding."

She ran to the fire station. "Look what someone has done," she told deputy chief officer Joseph Smith, showing a cut in her sleeve and two superficial wounds to her arm. Smith noticed that she didn't seem too distressed – unlike the mob of several hundred people who soon appeared at the scene to search for the attacker.

A police statement the next morning: "This is more a matter of exciting and alarming the public. The victims are not badly hurt. There is no doubt that the person or persons concerned are getting tremendous satisfaction from the publicity that has been obtained. Anything the able-bodied public can do to patrol their own districts will be appreciated by the authorities. Such patrols should use the phone boxes and flash any news to headquarters. This town, like all industrial towns, lends itself to the disappearance trick. It is inadvisable for womenfolk to go out without proper escort and they would be well advised to keep away from side streets and dark places. It is not thought that it is a mental case. It is sheer devilment. There is probably more than one person concerned probably about three."

Three days later, Sorrell was one of the first women to confess: "I did it myself after having a row with my boy." She'd had to beg the tuppence bus fare home off Higgins before abandoning him to the Prince of Wales pub. She spent half on a new razor blade, Mick Lee brand. "I held hold of the blade in my right hand and slashed down my left arm, making a long cut in my mackintosh coat and cardigan. I then put the blade back into the cut, and scratched down my arm twice... I put my fingers through the cut in the cloth and saw that they were covered in blood. The reason why I cut my arm was because I was in a temper, and had been reading in the papers about girls being slashed." Sorrell was sent for trial and received a sentence of four weeks. She was also said to have recently discovered that she was pregnant.

The far end of Bedford Street North comes out on Pellon Lane. After the Victorian lanes of west Halifax, the dolloping of generic retail sheds feels oddly disconcerting, like a sudden invasion from some other suburban world. Just up the road is The Running Man, a 1970s hutch of a pub named after a unique escapee of the Gibbet. In 1617, John Lacey escaped before the blade could fall and fled over the Hebble Brook, the parish boundary, to freedom. Lacey optimistically returned to Halifax in early 1623, but a rapid arrest and execution soon relieved him of the notion that he'd been pardoned.

Annoyingly, the pub sign shows the wrong kind of gibbet – a generic cage for exhibiting a miscreant's corpse.

Between The Running Man and entrance to a B&Q looms the five-storey, vaguely Italianite wedge of Martins Mill, behind which ran a now-vanished street called Green Lane and the Stannery neighbourhood. It was here on the evening of 25 November that Hilda Lodge left her house at Upper Dennis Gallery to buy a penn'orth of vinegar for her evening chips. Lodge, 35 years old, had been in poor health with her nerves and was chary of walking the poorly-lit path back to her house. As she related it: "I'm not too keen about going up there, and I was singing to reassure myself as I walked up. Just as I got to the corner, an arm came round the wall-side and aimed a blow at me."

Lodge dropped her decanter and ran to the house of her neighbour, Mrs Whitaker. Moaning and semi-conscious, she had cuts to her face and forearm, which soon proved to be much less serious than they first looked. The real trouble was outside. Clifford George Edwards had left his house in Pellon Lane to join in the growing throng of concerned citizens, but found himself at the wrong end of mob justice. Momentarily separated from the main body of searchers, he was pounced upon with a shout of "Here he is!" Edwards found himself at the centre of an angry crowd, surrounded by cries reported as "Kill the b——!" and "Break his b—— neck!" He was saved by the police officers attending to Hilda Lodge, and escorted back home.

Lodge confessed to faking her attack on the same day as Beatrice Sorrell: "I don't know what made me do it. Will it get into the papers if I tell you what happened?" She told police: "It has made my nerves worse since I done it... I have always suffered with my nerves and last week I read a lot in the papers about people being slashed with razors. This seemed to get on top of me and I thought I would cut myself. I told newspapermen a lot of lies. I am sorry for all the trouble I have caused, but it is all through my nerves, from which I have suffered for some years." She received the standard four week sentence.

Lodge was the fourth apparent victim of the Slasher that night. Minutes before she left the house and some five miles to the south, Percy Waddington, manager of the Halifax Co-operative Industrial Society grocery store in Elland, was returning home with fish and chips after a trip to the pub. "I don't really know a great deal about it. I never heard a thing. I felt a cut across my hand, and, turning around, grabbed. I didn't know I had anything in my hand until I went into the house of some friends near by." Waddington had managed to grab a tab from the assailant's mackintosh, and later found a Corrux razor blade close by a pool of blood. It was the first real clue to the Slasher's identity.

Except the next day, a raincoat was found on the Old Earth rugby union ground just opposite Waddington's shop – a coat with a missing cuff tab. A former Co-op errand boy soon identified the coat as Waddington's own, and on the evening of 29 November he confessed faking the attack, the first "victim" to own up. He told police: "I don't know what came over me, but I took out a safety razor blade from my pocket and cut my left hand across the back... I am very sorry I have caused the police all this trouble. I realise I have been a fool, but get very excited and sometimes don't know what I am doing. It had been on my mind about all those other attacks in the district. I am not responsible for those slashing attacks." He was charged with effecting a public mischief and bound over for three years.

Behind Martins Mill and the B&Q run three blocks of flats, built to replace some the worst terraced slums on

Green Lane and other lost streets. The most foetid areas of back-to-back terraces were already being cleared in the 1930s. June 1938 saw the opening of the Odeon cinema on Broad Lane, off the foot of Pellon Lane on the site of the Cross Fields slums. The art deco cinema, Halifax's largest at a time when cinema dominated the town's entertainment, is now a bingo hall – with typical sensitivity to the town's Muslims, a Mecca.

These pale brown blocks, known as the Crib Lane flats after one almost vanished road, have themselves decayed into near slums, vertical now rather than horizontal. Replete with asbestos, they now await demolition.

Crib Lane was the scene of a shocking murder in July 1926, when 22-year-old William Cornelius Jones shot his wife Winifred. She was 18, eight months pregnant, and beginning divorce proceedings on grounds of cruelty. As she lay dying, he was heard to tell her: "I have done it. You have no need to be frightened. I shan't run away." Jones was hanged at Leeds that winter.

Also down here is the local police headquarters, a modern block hung with banners: "Target / fighting crime / fighting the fear of crime". Maybe something in the town inspired the first notions of policing – Robert Peel attended Hipperholme Grammar School just to the east of Halifax. The founder of the modern police force, Peel also introduced the word "Conservative" into British politics. An earlier Hipperholme alumnus was Laurence Sterne, creator of the pre-emptive postmodernism of *Tristram Shandy*.

Across the dual carriageway of Ovenden Road curls the surviving remnant of Crib Lane, a cobbled wind down to the massive Dean Clough mill complex. On 28 November 1938, a crowd broke down the iron gates of Bowling Dyke Mill, on the far side of the complex, and through the stone door of a shed in their search for the Slasher. A vertiginous flight of steps provides a shorter way down, and the location for the final attack of the Slasher panic.

On 29 November 1938, Detective Chief Inspector William Salisbury and Sergeant Harry Studdard arrived in Halifax from Scotland Yard. Salisbury was known as "the terror of the North London toughs", and the man who smashed the London razor gangs. The *Courier*: "Halifax has certainly never had such a man hunt in its history, and the hunt generally is probably unparalleled since the days of the Jack the Ripper scare in London."

From the paper's *The Trend of Things* column that day:

"Not within living memory has Halifax been so worked up as it is over the series of slashing affairs, which has resulted in the calling in of Scotland Yard. Just over a week ago, when the first of these Halifax outrages occurred, none could anticipate that the slashings would assume such proportions as has now been the case, or that they would have had such a marked effect on so many of the normal activities of a town that is usually free from sensation – which, of course, is another way of saying that it is a town both well-governed and well-behaved. Somehow, Halifax people have got used to reading about violence and other horrors happening elsewhere – but not in Halifax. Now Halifax is receiving national notoriety of a kind the cause of which is a matter for nothing but regret, and there is only one topic of conversation wherever one goes – the slasher."

The *Courier* also found it necessary to counter suggestions that the victims were almost entirely Roman Catholic, and that there was "some religious animus in these attacks".

On the evening of the 29th, Mary Kenny, a 40-year-old of Back Crib Lane, descended the Crib Lane steps to check the time by the clock visible through the window of the mill building to the left. It was 7.20.

"He attacked me from behind as I was coming up the steps leading to Crib-lane, and first of all he gripped me by the left arm, while at the same time he made several cuts in my right arm just below the elbow. I am a fairly strong woman – I have heavy work to do – and I held on to him for what seemed to be two or three minutes. I dared not scream because I felt I had the chance of holding him until someone came. If I had screamed he would have run away. But no-one came and I realised that I should be badly hurt if I did not give the alarm. I screamed and immediately he released me and ran away." A few men who appeared on the scene gave chase, but failed to catch up.

Later that night, Percy Waddington confessed all to the gents from Scotland Yard. The panic began to wind down, although vigilante groups still patrolled the town for a few days, and odd claims of attack still came in. On the evening of 30 November, claims of attack by a "dark figure" on one Nellie Widdop in Villiers Street, now the site of the Madni Mosque, was immediately dismissed by the police.

The same night on Gibbet Street, a 36-year-old cripple called Jimmy Fawcett claimed to have menaced by a man in a dark coat and trilby who came at him "grimacing and grinning". Fawcett screamed and helpers came running – one was promptly chased as a likely suspect by a patrol that also rushed to the scene.

Reports of Slasher attacks came in from as far afield as Glasgow and London but, on 2 December, the *Halifax Courier* sounded the all-clear:

"Carry on Halifax, the slashing scare is over! The theory that a half-crazed, wild-eyed man has been wandering around, attacking helpless women in dark streets, is exploded. The Chief Constable of Halifax, Mr.

A. H. Richardson, to-day recommended the public 'to carry out without further fear their normal domestic shopping, entertainment, and social interest.' It is now being accepted that while there are some cases still to be properly investigated, a work that may yet take some weeks, 'There never was, nor is there likely to be in this connection, any real danger to the general public.' There is no doubt that following certain happenings public feeling has grown, and that many small incidents have been magnified in the public mind until a real state of alarm was caused. The assurance that there is no real cause for alarm, in short, no properly authenticated wholesale attacks by such a person as the bogy man known as the 'Slasher', should now allay public fear."

The panic was over, but an explanation of "mass hysteria" was no explanation at all. A fortnight later at the first hearings for public mischief, prosecuting solicitor HN Curtis: "It is almost inconceivable that sane persons should do injury to themselves and then wilfully make reports to the police which are false. It is not for the prosecution, however, to prove motive. You may think that in some cases persons were actuated by sheer wilfullness, or a perverted desire to gain cheap publicity, or a form of hysteria induced by some neurotic condition, or by a combination of such mentalities."

While some of the victims confessed and were prosecuted, others – including Mary Sutcliffe, Clayton Aspinall and Mary Kenny – were not. Were they really attacked? Was there a genuine razor-wielding maniac on the loose? Or was the climate of fear prompting some to pick up razors and enact attacks on others, just as it was prompting others to cut themselves in a Munchausen's cry for attention? And why Halifax, and why November 1938?

The questions are worth pondering as you drop down into Dean Clough. The kilometre-long complex, formerly the largest carpet mill in the world, has been painstakingly regenerated as a centre for business and the arts. Its developer, Sir Ernest Hall, calls it a "practical utopia" – call centres, those dark satanic mills of the information age, cohabit with web designers and artists' studios. The place is full of surprises, from alien-head sculptures peeping through ivy to the five reserved parking places for The Hospitaller Order of St John of God. There's also the Northern Broadsides theatre group, reinventing Greek tragedies in broad Yorkshire. Recent productions include new translations of Oedipus and Antigone by Blake Morrison, writer of *The Ballad of the Yorkshire Ripper*.

Alan Moore, the Northampton gnostic of comics and magick, invoked the Halifax Slasher in his dissection of the Whitechapel murders, *From Hell*. Borrowing from James Hinton, he postulated an architecture of history, "an invisible curve, rising through the centuries".

In 1788, the London Monster terrorised the capital, slicing through women's clothing and skin. One hundred years later, Jack the Ripper stalked the East End. Fifty years after that, the Halifax Slasher. Another twenty-five years, Ian Brady and Myra Hindley are burying their child victims just over the hills at Saddleworth. Twelve and a half years after that, Peter Sutcliffe starts hearing the voices.

It's an elegant theory, marred only by the failure of this murderous apocalypse to noticeably crescendo in 1988.

The Halifax case is the joker in the pack, as Moore notes: "In my more fanciful and speculative moments, it seems almost as though whatever dark cthonic energies led to the crimes of Whitechapel and elsewhere was unable to find a suitable receptacle in Halifax, leaving a vortex of panic and mutilation with an almost mystic absence at the centre."

Perhaps those energies just missed their receptacle. In December 1938, John Reginald Halliday Christie moved into 10 Rillington Place, fourteen years after leaving his Halifax home. Born at Shibden, he moved with his family to Boothtown, the model community on Haley Hill above Dean Clough. As a child, his bedroom overlooked the graveyard of All Souls' Church, and his father worked as a carpet designer at the mills below.

A steep cobbled lane leads up from the back of Dean Clough to the densest part of Boothtown. Christie's wife, Ethel Simpson Waddington, lived here on Woodside Crescent. He moved to London in 1924 after a few petty convictions in Halifax, and Ethel followed him a decade later.

Five years after they moved to Rillington Place, Christie began strangling and gassing their tenants and, in 1952, his wife.

The story was popularised by the 1970 film *10 Rillington Place*, starring Richard Attenborough as Christie. Attenborough's other great psychopath role was as the razor-wielding Pinky Brown in *Brighton Rock*, based on the Graham Greene novel published in 1938.

The Yorkshire Ripper also made an early visit to Boothtown. On 15 August 1975, 46-year-old Olive Smelt was returning from an evening in town. Her friends dropped her off on Boothtown Road, and she took a short cut down a ginnel. She was followed by Peter Sutcliffe, who had earlier seen her drinking in a pub. The last she heard: "Weather's letting us down, isn't it?" Sutcliffe smashed her head, and slashed at her back with a knife. Interrupted, Sutcliffe returned to his car where his friend Trevor Birdsall innocently waited. Smelt survived, one of the lucky ones.

A more recent incident is as odd as anything in the saga of the phantom Slasher. On 28 January 2003, Adrian Marsden, the newly elected British National Party councillor for Mixenden, claimed he was attacked by two men in black close to his home on Woodside Terrace. One wore a long trench coat, the other a suit and tie. Both wore leather gloves. At a press conference, Marsden declared that the men were "government special agents" or thugs "hired by the Labour Party" – they were clearly not from Halifax because they were "professionally dressed and had educated accents".

As in the 1930s, the extreme right is on the rise, thriving on rumours and fears about the outsider. Oswald Mosley's British Union of Fascists, with backing from the *Daily Mail*, had some of its strongest support in the mill towns of Yorkshire and Lancashire – less so in Halifax than in many of the surrounding towns, but there may well have been blackshirts among the patrols of Slasher vigilantes.

Marsden's election in Mixenden was followed by that of his election agent Richard Mulhall in Illingworth and the defection of Illingworth Conservative councillor Geoffrey Wallace. Marsden himself has been linked to Combat 18, the BNP's former "security" wing named for the initials of Adolf Hitler, and had his Boothtown home raided by Special Branch in March 1999. A few months after his election, he informed a Labour councillor: "Woman or no, I'm going to level you."

Marsden was elected on the back of a campaign playing on fears of asylum seekers, the latest enemy within and tabloid phantom menace. Isolated from the town a few miles up the Keighley road, Mixenden itself is physically dominated by the run-down and isolated Jumples estate, an overwhelmingly white displaced counterpart to the poorest parts of west Halifax, the kind of place where gritting trucks get stoned off the roads in winter. But the ward is much larger and, contrary to the assumptions of the national reporters who rushed to the scene following the BNP's win, the bulk of the fascist vote came from the surrounding communities at the expense of the Conservatives – respectable folk fearing encroachment. One such village is Mount Tabor, named for the Biblical site overlooking the Valley of Armageddon.

For the BNP voters, the threat is seated in the Asian communities of west Halifax. The streets where residents lived in fear of the Slasher for a few weeks are now known as a no-go area for many people who've never been there. In July 2001, rumours started circulating round west Halifax about an attack by the National Front, the more openly racist group whose continuing links with the BNP remain ambiguous. Shops were closed, children brought home from school, but the violence for once failed to materialise. This was just a few days after the Bradford riots, sparked by a handful of NF agitators, and the biggest recruiting boost the BNP could have hoped for.

Since the BNP entered the council, the town has become more tense. There's a definite sense of waiting for something to happen, something to break. Suspicious looks, lowered voices, pissed-up beatings in the town centre every weekend. It's nothing new.

Coming back into town, beneath the concrete towers of the Burdock Way flyover lies the old North Bridge. On 15 August 1842, probably the largest mob ever seen in Halifax began with a procession of four or five thousand Chartist marchers entering across this bridge from Bradford, a famished-looking mob armed with bludgeons, flails, pitchforks and pikes. Five thousand more entered the town from Skircoat Moor, where they'd spent the night. That group had come across from Lancashire, swelling in number as it came, closing the mills as it went by drawing the plugs from the boilers. They entered Halifax singing Chartist hymns and the 100th Psalm: "Make a joyful noise unto the Lord, all ye lands." The two groups met and the Riot Act was read. At the height, a mob of some 25,000 people thronged the streets of Halifax.

Nineteenth century Halifax was no stranger to riot, with street disturbances involving Irish immigrants a regular occurrence. During the elections of 1806–07, a detachment of Inniskillen dragoons was despatched to the town to quell disturbances at election meetings. The *Halifax Journal* reported "a riotous and desperate mob" carrying effigies of the slave-owning Whig candidate Henry Lascelles, and concluded that "nothing since the days of the Revolution has ever presented such a scene".

North Bridge was also the scene of angry confrontations during the carters' strike riots of 1913, where strikers and police fought over a dray laden with toffee tins for the Mackintosh factory.

But in July 1981, the *Ghost Town* summer of riots, Halifax mustered one of the least impressive: a pissed-up mob of 300, smashing windows, chanting "Riot, riot, we want a riot." Chief Inspector Malcolm Thompson: "This was not in any way racial. It was the local idiots who were getting stirred up in licensed premises in the town centre."

Coming into town, you enter one of the best preserved Victorian town centres in Yorkshire, the shop fronts now mostly blasted clean of the black smog residues. The modern town is defined by what has gone before, fragments of odd history that may give further clues to the mystery of the Slasher.

The town hall still dominates all. From a design by Charles Barry, architect of the London Parliament, and completed by his son, the hall opened in 1863. Built in local stone, it's a High Victorian confection of columns, angels and lions, heads of Wisdom, Justice and Mercy, and stern inspirational slogans: "Delay not to do well"; "Be just and fear not"; "The night cometh".

The interior is, if anything, even more impressive. It served as location for the 1959 film of *Room at the Top*, based on the first novel by Bradford-born John Braine. Braine's second novel, *The Vodi*, was a unique kitchen-sink gothic about a phantom conspiracy in a Yorkshire town: "The Vodi were all alike, small and ferret-faced with no more identity than amoebae. There wasn't really such a thing as a Vodi; there was only the Vodi."

A hundred-odd BNP supporters surrounded the town hall as Marsden's election was announced, singing *Rule Britannia* before Marsden was whisked away in a white van. An anti-racist demo five months later also finished with a rally here – photos of the crowd soon appeared on the *Redwatch* website with exhortations to teach these "traitors" a violent lesson.

Further into town on Market Street, the Portman & Pickles pub, nestling in the corner of the glass-roofed Borough Market, commemorates two local celebrities of the war years.

Eric Portman is the actor best known for his Nazi u-boat captain in *49th Parallel* and his Number Two in the *Free For All* episode of *The Prisoner*. His first major film role was alongside Tod Slaughter in *The Murder in the Red Barn*, but his strangest was in Powell and Pressburger's wartime parable *A Canterbury Tale*. Portman played a respectable magistrate who turns out to be the "Glue Man", a shadowy, near-mythical mystery man who attacks local girls. The role had been refused by Powell and Pressburger's usual leading man, Roger Livesey – did Portman feel some personal affinity?

Wilfred Pickles meanwhile became the first national newsreader with a pronounced northern accent in December 1941, signing off each night with a hearty "Good-neet". His appointment was a strategic decision by minister of information Brendan Bracken to foil Nazi propagandists, who had become expert at imitating BBC Oxford accents. Pickles also acted in films, with roles including the father of Tom Courtenay's smalltown fantasist in *Billy Liar*.

Just down from the market is the Piece Hall, the last building of its kind still standing in Britain. Opened in 1779 as a trading hall for the local weavers and wool merchants, it's a wide sloping piazza surrounded by Romanesque arcades, the weavers' box-like rooms now selling quirky oddments, collectible tat, secondhand books and records.

At the Westgate entrance, beneath a paschal lamb impaled on a weather vane, the stone wall is imprinted with an inexplicable handprint. The story is of a 19th century murderer fleeing pursuit who pressed his hands onto the grimy wall, his guilt leaving an irremovable mark on the stone.

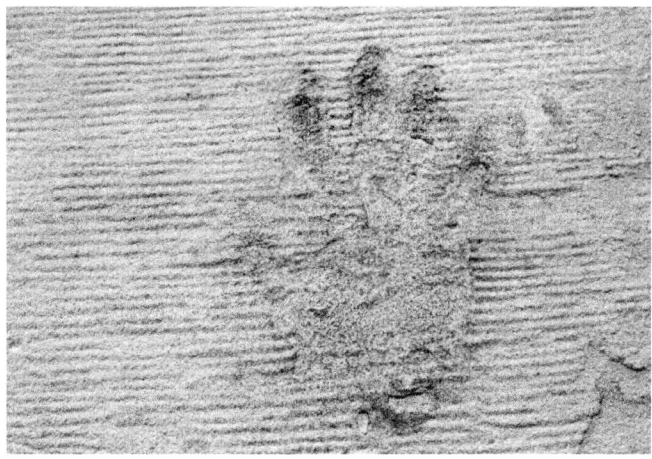

At the south gate, huge and ornate cast iron gates carry four replicas of the Halifax Coat of Arms, with the head of John the Baptist and the town motto: "Nisi Dominus custodierit civitatem". The motto comes from the 127th Psalm: "Except the Lord keep the city, the watchman waketh but in vain."

To the east, the gothic spire of the fire-gutted Square Congregational Church looks over the red brick Square Chapel, built in 1772 to Masonic principles, in the shape of Solomon's Temple.

Beyond that, the steep slope of Beacon Hill truncates Halifax's sprawl, leaving the town permanently lopsided. The hill is crossed by the ancient Wakefield Gate pathway, and in the 18th century hosted the suspended bodies of executed men as a moral warning for the town below.

Coming back up through the town, the dark glass wedge of the Halifax bank headquarters squats on its concrete pillars like a visitor from some forgotten *Logan's Run* future. The local rumour is that there's as much of it below the ground as above.

The Coliseum nightclub next door marks the end of the town's infamous Booze Ring, a place of necessary pilgrimage for anyone seeking an energetic if unsophisticated night on the Dionysian lash. At the heart of the Booze Ring at Bull Green, Winston Churchill addressed a crowd of 20,000 during his post-war election campaign.

There's also a bench here dedicated to the memory of Ralph Fox: "Writer / Friend of the people / Soldier for liberty".

Born in Halifax in 1900, Fox was a political writer and novelist who, like Orwell and others of his generation, enlisted in the International Brigades in 1936. Shortly before, he wrote:

"It is our fortune to have been born at one of those moments in history which demand from each one of us as an individual that he make his private decision... We are a part of that spiritual community with the dead of which Wordsworth spoke, we cannot stand aside, and by our actions we shall extend our imagination, because we shall have been true to the passions in us."

He was killed in the first days of 1937, under heavy fire from Franco's fascists and German Junkers, in the hills of Andalusia.

Less than two years after Fox's death, his home town spasmed, turning against itself and the phantom Slasher in its midst.

Fox: "The best human beings are liable to become

entangled in the terrible network of contradictions in which they live and their life becomes a torment of doubts and frustrated desires."

Less than a year later Halifax, and all of Britain, was at war with fascism. It's as good a place as any to stop the walk, at this small memorial to the fight, driven by idealism or survival, against that uncompromising political expression of the same hysteria and violence that birthed the Halifax Slasher.

In part by their apathy, in part by their passivity, and in part actively, these masses of people make possible the catastrophes under which they themselves suffer more than anybody else. To stress this guilt on the part of masses of people, to hold them solely responsible, means to take them seriously. On the other hand, to commiserate masses of people as victims, means to treat them as small, helpless children.

> Wilhelm Reich, *The Mass Psychology of Fascism*

Acknowledgements

Most of the information on the Slasher attacks is taken from *The Halifax Slasher: An urban terror in the north of England* by Michael Goss (Fortean Times Occasional Paper no.3, 1987); and from contemporary reports in the *Halifax Daily Courier and Guardian*, as preserved in the archives at Halifax Central Library.

For points of the town's history, *Halifax* by John A Hargreaves (Edinburgh University Press, 1999) and *The Story of Old Halifax* by TW Hanson (1920; reprinted by MTD Rigg Publications, 1993) were invaluable, as were the websites associated with the *Halifax Evening Courier*.

The path of this walk was hacked out during two leisurely strolls in July 2002 and November 2003 with Mr Barry Kavanagh, whose screenplay based on the Slasher panic inspired several trains of thought.

OLD HAUNTS REVISITED

1. Before and afterlife

Fifteen years have passed since I wrote *Haunts of the Halifax Slasher*, a third of my life. The world has changed, and the town has changed.

I became interested in the Slasher phenomenon soon after moving to Halifax in 2000. It was the town's unique geography that brought me there – driving almost at random out of Manchester in summer 1999, looking for somewhere to live on the right side of the Pennines, the gothic finger of Wainhouse Tower beckoned me along the valley and up the hill.

Arriving at Savile Park, this immediately felt like a good place. The town centre seemed prosperous and at peace – certainly in comparison to where I was then living, a cheaply converted mill in Miles Platting. (It was years later that I discovered that the same mill makes an iconic appearance in the film of *A Taste of Honey*, and was also a stone's throw from the ruined church and slum clearance site at the start of Alan Garner's *Elidor*, a childhood favourite.)

Shortly after I moved into a sturdy Victorian terrace at Bell Hall, I was sent a copy of Michael Goss's monograph on the Slasher by Mark Pilkington, a friend from London working at the *Fortean Times*. I realised that many of the key sites of the 1938 panic were just a short distance on the other side of King Cross, an area I'd already started to explore as I visited the Queens Road antique centre for furniture to fill my new abode.

In 2002, I was contacted by another fortean pal, Barry Kavanagh, who was working on a speculative screenplay about the Slasher. Barry visited a couple of times and we toured the sites with the Goss as guide, driving out to Barkisland and Elland as well as visiting the Standard of Freedom at Skircoat (location of a Slasher-hunting mob attack on 15-year-old Fred Baldwin), and walking through the western side of the town to Dean Clough, plotting the course for the essay to come.

Around this time, Mark published the first *Strange Attractor Journal*, which included Drew Mulholland (of Mt Vernon Arts Lab fame) on the psychic landscaping of his native Glasgow. Mark said that he'd like a regional psychogeographic piece in each volume, and I offered to write what became *Haunts of the Halifax Slasher*.

I'd been reading Iain Sinclair since 1991, buying *White Chappell, Scarlet Tracings* after Alan Moore and Grant Morrison produced their graphic homages. I'd then read Stewart Home and the provocations of the London Psychogeographical Association while living in Hackney in the late '90s. Psychogeography was then predominantly a London pursuit: *Haunts* was in part an attempt to bring its approach, as I understood it, out to the real Britain.

The journal launched with a memorable evening in London's Horse Hospital, featuring what is still my only attempt at public poetry reading (see p58). After publication, there was limited but positive feedback on the piece. After a decent interval, I posted *Haunts* to the website I used for my freelance work, where it had a long tail of interest.

The most rewarding comments came years later, when one or two other local writers said it had influenced the way they approached the mysteries of the West Riding. In 2017, the much-garlanded Benjamin Myers acknowledged it ("the most thorough and informative point of research...") in his own anti-crime novel of a mystery assailant panic in modern-day Hebden Bridge, *These Darkening Days*.

I also led a guided tour of the haunts on a few occasions, for visiting friends or interested parties such as John Davies, a Merseyside vicar on his own Sinclair-inspired exploration along the path of the M62 in September 2007.

And when I started using Twitter towards the end of the decade, I took *@HalifaxSlasher* for an identity. I wanted something that would provide some degree of anonymity, but would be obvious to a small set of friends.

The years passed. Some of the specifics of the piece became dated – Ralph Fox's bench was moved into the Piece Hall, which then shut for restorations; the Portman & Pickles became the Jubilee. The electoral success of the BNP decayed among the usual factional squabbling and crankiness, while their rhetoric and intolerance gradually contaminated politics across the country. The new tone had been set by the 2005 Conservative campaign slogan, which lingered after the election on a tattered poster at the top of Dean Clough: "Are you thinking what we're thinking?"

The banking crisis hit Halifax hard. The summer of 2008 brought HBOS to the brink, the innovative financial engineering that followed the 2001 merger collapsing into the vaults of bad mortgages. Fears of job cuts that would devastate families across the town, crunch meetings, long-lensed press photographers loitering around the

Trinity Street HQ. In the end, the government stepped in to arrange an emergency acquisition by Lloyds. The town lost what senior jobs and sway had survived the earlier merger, but – maybe coincidentally – did gain a long-sought direct rail link to London.

As the new decade began, the austerity coalition cut hard and cruel. Calderdale Council lost over 55 per cent of its annual core funding (in real terms, even more) in the decade since 2010. Shops and services closed, the town got rougher. The family next door to us sold up, and the end-terrace house became a rental property for an absent landlord. Kids ran along the slate roofs of the terrace, cars were scratched up along the street. We moved out in 2013.

2. Return of the repressed

I went back on occasion, of course, but didn't revisit the Slasher sites until late in 2019. I was contacted by a historian, Dr John Woolf, and radio producer, Nick Baker, who were working on an audiobook about the whole phenomenon. I agreed to show them around, and add my thoughts to the mix.

If you believed the press, Halifax had enjoyed something of a renaissance in the past few years. The Piece Hall reopened on Yorkshire Day 2017, and something resembling a hipster scene flowered around the Victorian Craft Beer Café and Grayston Unity bar. A BBC 6Music DJ from the other side of the Pennines had used the phrase "Shoreditch of the North", and the local tourism promoters had overlooked any intended irony. (My personal view, having lived in Shoreditch in the late 1990s, is that it isn't necessarily a state to aspire to.) And just a couple of days before I met with John and Nick, the *Guardian* had hailed Halifax as the new global hub of lesbian tourism, thanks to the *Gentleman Jack* fame of Anne Lister and Shibden Hall.

We met on 20 November, the day before the anniversary of the first Slasher attack on Mary Sutcliffe. The general election was in three weeks, though there was little sign of any campaigning activity in the streets. This election was being fought virtually, in misconceived photo opportunities and social media trolling, in accusations and rumours and outright lies. This was a moment when even the concept of truth seemed as antiquated as a gaberdine raincoat or Corrux razor.

This election had been called by a minority government with a violent contempt for reality and for anyone who didn't fit with their views, under the impossible flag of getting Brexit done. We seemed to be a nation intent on self harm, driven mad by tensions we couldn't honestly face.

Halifax voted 59 per cent for Leave in the 2016 referendum, above the average for Yorkshire. The murder of Jo Cox by a violent right-winger, 10 miles away in Birstall, hadn't shifted the mood but had inspired a barrage of copycat threats to troublesome female MPs.

For the ill-advised general election of 2017, Theresa May launched the Conservative campaign in Halifax with the promise of "mainstream government that will deliver for mainstream Britain". It didn't go too well for them. Halifax remained Labour, but was now seen as a marginal battleground. Now, the Conservatives were ahead in the national polls, but the pundits reckoned that local variables and peculiarities across an increasingly divided nation made predictions worthless. It seemed that this sleazy fog of lies, intimidation and fantasy was what we wanted.

Walking from our rendezvous at the Phoenix FM studios in Dean Clough, we pause beneath concrete pillars to admire the town's particular geography. Literally, it works on many levels: the Hebble brook below, tamed by the first wave of industrialisation; the Victorian wrought iron of North Bridge at our level; all dwarfed by the brutalist curves of the Burdock Way flyover.

We pass the towering wall of the new cinema and its associated leisure opportunities, and onto the bottom end of Lister Lane before doglegging back to the Gibbet Street bridge over the cut of the dual carriageway.

Coming this way, it's clear how the neighbourhoods of west Halifax have been cut off from the centre by this inner relief road, opened in 1973 as part of an unfulfilled masterplan to create a motorway town fit for a white heat future. It's even more of a barrier to the pedestrian than the Huddersfield ring road, a more recent locus of interest – two months earlier, I'd led a walking exploration of the Huddersfield Orbital as part of the Fourth World Congress of Psychogeography.

We come back to Lister Lane, walking up between the cemetery (now largely cleared of its erstwhile rampant undergrowth) and the back of the Crossley mansion and its attendant almhouses. I'm struck anew by how Francis Street must have originally been a distinctly salubrious neighbourhood, high-Victorian mansions, churches and wide terraced townhouses for the emerging middle classes. Myrtle Dene, the stonework marked JW for the local Waterhouse gentry, is now the Al-Jamia Al-Zahra mosque and largely hidden from the street by black wrought fencing with gold spikes, red and green flowers.

Sutcliffe's home on Allerton Street and its neighbouring terraces – smaller back-to-back and through houses, according to the reprinted map of 1905 which we were using to navigate – have long gone, though there's plenty of similar streets remaining to give the visitors a flavour of this closeknit landscape.

As we record a piece to microphone by the mostly shut-up industrial units that replaced the Allerton lanes, a car rolls up with a vigilant local. The middle-aged Asian driver asks what we're doing, and listens carefully as the producer tries to explain. He hasn't heard of the Slasher, but vaguely recalls a caretaker and a murder at the church on Francis Street. He says he'll google it.

A similar thing happened on my first visit here with Barry Kavanagh – a car full of younger Asian men rolled up as we discussed the scene on Lister Lane. They seemed more suspicious in asking what we were up to. We said something about a history project, and they seemed content enough when I assured them that I was local. On that occasion, we quickly headed back down the hill to town.

In 2019, we continue up to Queens Road and cross to the former School of Art. It's a bleak scene, everything run down even further from what I remember.

On Jasper Street, on the spot where Clayton Aspinall experienced his violent collision, a middle-aged white man loads gas cylinders from Bibby's works into a white van. On the other side, a mixed gaggle of teenagers in baseball caps and trackies smoke by the side of the former school. They call mocking greetings, but nothing more. We don't linger long.

We head back down Gibbet Street to the gibbet itself, the reconstructed engine now accompanied by an information board explaining the history. We're joined by what seem to be actual tourists – two women, perhaps members of the international Listerhood.

There's a bass thud of music from location unknown, an anxious heartbeat of rhythm. We shelter in the lee of the Dunelm shed, next to rat traps, to record our piece about the unfortunate Beatrice Sorrell.

We dodge the traffic to cross Pellon Lane, below a newly renovated Martins Mill which now offers 60 one and two-bedroom flats, marketed by Propertyfrontiers as "our latest buy-to-let hotspot investment".

On the steps into the car park for the former B&Q, now The Range, we survey what remains of the Stannary neighbourhood where Hilda Lodge made her vinegary cuts. The slums that were cleared and rebuilt last century have now been cleared again, the Crib Lane high-rises a fenced-off plain of rubble.

On the final leg back to Dean Clough, I take the wrong underpass and cross beneath the wrong road, away from our intended destination. It's been too long: I've lost my native direction.

Curling back to the Crib Lane steps, the scene has changed again. The old mill block has been refurbished as offices, the stonework blasted to a clean gold, new stainless steel railings in place of the old black and rust. It's beginning to get dark on this cold November day, and I reckon it's still the most atmospheric location of the 1938 panic.

I used to say, only half as a joke, that if you wanted to reshoot *The Exorcist* in Halifax, you'd shoot here. But in 2019, it also brings to mind one of this year's cinematic icons – Joaquin Phoenix's *Joker*. Another version of a character from pulp comics of the late 1930s, with roots in older fictions (the razor-slashed grin of *The Man Who Laughs*), borrowing heavily from Alan Moore's *Killing Joke* of 1988 (the year when *From Hell*'s invisible curve of murder was supposed to reach its apogee). This new film posited surreal acts of violence as a reasonable response to unbearable social pressures, and the media fretted about its ability to inspire copycat crimes.

We tap down the steps to our end.

THE BALLAD OF
THE HALIFAX SLASHER

A found poem comprising headlines in the *Halifax Daily Courier and Guardian*, 17 November – 5 December 1938.

This poem was performed at the launch party for *Strange Attractor Journal* vol. 2, at The Horse Hospital in London in the summer of 2005, and published online at *strangeattractor.co.uk*.

Girls' struggle with assailant in dark local lane.
Theory of hatchet or mallet.
Head wounds which required stitches;
Brutal attack at Ripponden.

Police all-night patrol of district.
Womenfolk's uneasiness.

Mystery of night attack
on young woman in Halifax street.
Wrist wound from sharp instrument;
Put her arm up to ward off blow.
Incident near gas lamp.

£10 police reward for arrest
of Halifax Slasher.
Attack on man last night;
Caretaker's hand and head cut.
School of Art guarded by police;
Precautions taken for safety.

Two Slashers at work in district?
Time factor in last night's attacks:
Three at Halifax and one at Elland.
Special plans of police.

Halifax Slasher strikes
in darkness of early morning.
Police increase reward to £25.
Who is shielding the terror man?
Identity must be guessed
by someone.

Thin attendance at prize distribution;
Discord of Slasher affects music event.

Scotland Yard called in to help;
County, Bradford, Huddersfield
police co-operating.

Two more attacks on women last evening;
The first victim slashed again.

The Slasher: latest!
Danger of violence to innocent persons.
Hand over any suspects to the police.

Part of the cordon.
Outside the police station.
She went prepared.
With armlets and staff.

Elland mackintosh clue:
Owner traced by county police.
Halifax lull after Scotland Yard help;
No arrest yet made.

A Hull reflex:
Slasher scare affects fish shop trade.

No slashing attack yesterday – official.
Chief constable on misleading reports:
All incidents not associated with Slasher.
Protection for voters at tonight's polls.

Carry on Halifax!
The slashing scare is over.
Police chief's emphatic statement:
Never any real danger
to general public.
Court sequel expected tomorrow.

Elland man's alleged statement:
"I cut myself."
Remarkable evidence in mischief charge.

Halifax back to normal;
Public laughs off Slasher scare.
Is reward still open?

ABOUT THE AUTHOR

Tim Chapman lives in Yorkshire, and mostly writes about technology and business for a living.
His novel *Blue Shift* – a dark comedy about sex, drugs and evolutionary cosmology – was published in 2017.
Other work has appeared in *Strange Attractor Journal*, *Fortean Times*, *Ballardian.com* and books from RE/Search Publications.

Twitter: *@HalifaxSlasher*

Printed in Great Britain
by Amazon